That's Not Funny,
Charlie!

Written by Bridie Dickson

Illustrated by Ian Forss

Flying Start
to Literacy®

Contents

Chapter 1:
Charlie the prankster

Charlie loved to play pranks. Best of all, he loved to play pranks on his family.

One day, Charlie and his brother James were playing soccer. Suddenly, Charlie tripped on the ball and fell down.

"Ouch! Ouch!" yelled Charlie.
"My foot hurts!"

James ran to get help.

Charlie's mum came running.
She gently felt his foot.

Then Charlie smiled . . .

"Ha, ha! I fooled you!" he said.

"That's not funny, Charlie,"
said his mum. "Don't say you've hurt
yourself when you haven't. One day
you will get hurt and no one will
believe you."

But Charlie wasn't listening.

The next day, Charlie and James were helping Dad to make dinner.

"Ouch!" yelled Charlie.
"I've cut my finger!"

"Press down on the cut," said Dad.
"That will stop the bleeding."

Dad washed Charlie's finger . . .

"Ha, ha!" said Charlie. "I fooled you!"

"That's not funny," said Dad.
"One day you will get hurt and
no one will believe you."

Chapter 2:

One last prank

The next week, Charlie and James were visiting their grandmother.

"Just one last prank," said Charlie. "This will be my best prank ever!"

Charlie put some fake skin on his leg.

"Ouch!" yelled Charlie.
"Something has bitten me."

Grandma looked at Charlie's leg.
There were little red lumps all over it.
Grandma put an ice pack on his leg.

"Ouch! Ouch! Ouch!" said Charlie.
"My leg still hurts!"

"I'm taking you to the doctor, Charlie,"
said Grandma.

When the doctor pulled the fake skin off
his leg, Charlie tried not to smile . . .

but the doctor didn't smile.

"Charlie, one day you will really get
hurt and no one will believe you,"
said the doctor.

Chapter 3:
You can't fool us!

On the weekend, Charlie and his family went camping. They arrived at the camping ground and began to set up camp.

"I'll collect wood for our campfire," said Charlie.

Charlie ran down the side of the hill. He tripped and fell down.

"Ouch!" yelled Charlie. "My leg hurts."

Back at the camp, everyone could hear Charlie.

"You can't fool me this time, Charlie," said James.

"You can't fool us either," said Mum and Dad.

"And you can't fool me!" said Grandma.

"Help! Help!" yelled Charlie.
"I've really hurt my leg. I can't walk."

But still no one came to help Charlie.

"I will have to get back to camp by myself," said Charlie.

Charlie dragged himself up the side
of the hill.

"James," said Charlie, when he got to
the top. "Help me! I'm not pretending
this time."

But James was not sure.

James looked at Charlie's leg.
There was a big lump on Charlie's leg.

"He's not fooling!" yelled James.

Everyone rushed over to Charlie.
When they saw his leg, they knew
that he really was hurt this time.

"I think your leg is broken," said Mum.

"We will have to take you to hospital right now!" said Dad.

Chapter 4:
Charlie's promise

At the hospital, the doctor took an X-ray of Charlie's leg. It was broken.

Then the doctor put a cast on his broken leg.

"You're lucky that James believed you," said Dad.

"Yes, because we didn't," said Mum.

"I'm sorry," said Charlie. "I promise I will never pretend that I am hurt ever again."

And he never did . . .

But Charlie didn't promise to stop
playing pranks!